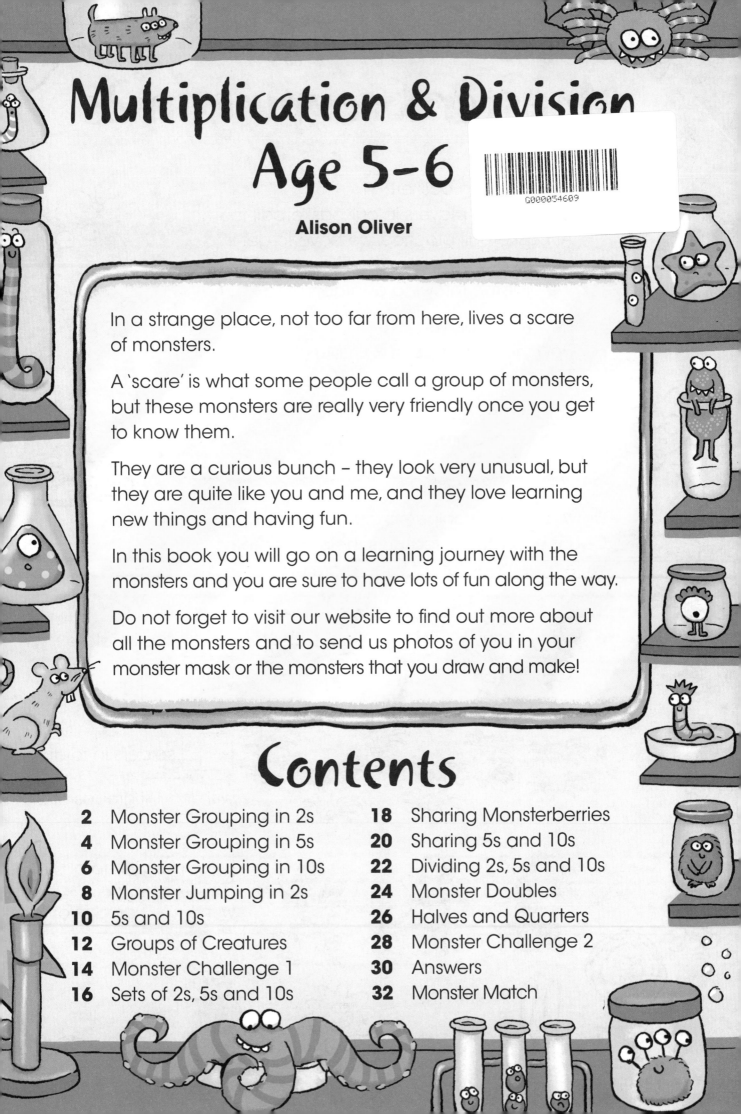

Multiplication & Division Age 5-6

Alison Oliver

In a strange place, not too far from here, lives a scare of monsters.

A 'scare' is what some people call a group of monsters, but these monsters are really very friendly once you get to know them.

They are a curious bunch – they look very unusual, but they are quite like you and me, and they love learning new things and having fun.

In this book you will go on a learning journey with the monsters and you are sure to have lots of fun along the way.

Do not forget to visit our website to find out more about all the monsters and to send us photos of you in your monster mask or the monsters that you draw and make!

Contents

Monster Grouping in 2s

> I love playing basketball.
> We have 10 players in our basketball team.
> At basketball practice, we have to get into groups of 2.
> We practise throwing and catching.
>
> How many players? 10
> How many **groups of 2** players? 5
> There are 5 groups of 2 in 10.
>
> Sometimes groups are called **lots**.
> Groups of 2 are called **pairs**.

1 Draw a different coloured circle around each group of 2.
Count how many creatures there are in total.
Write how many lots of 2 there are in total.

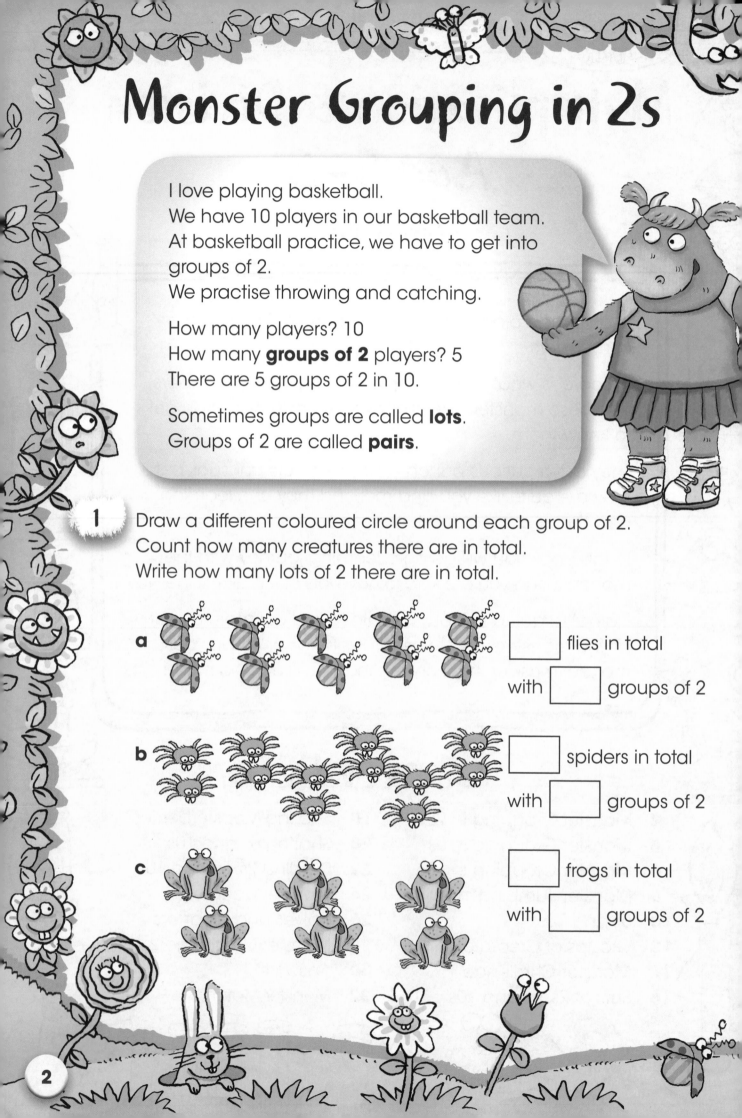

a ⬜ flies in total

with ⬜ groups of 2

b ⬜ spiders in total

with ⬜ groups of 2

c ⬜ frogs in total

with ⬜ groups of 2

2 Draw a circle around each pair of trainers.
Write how many 2s there are in each of these.

a 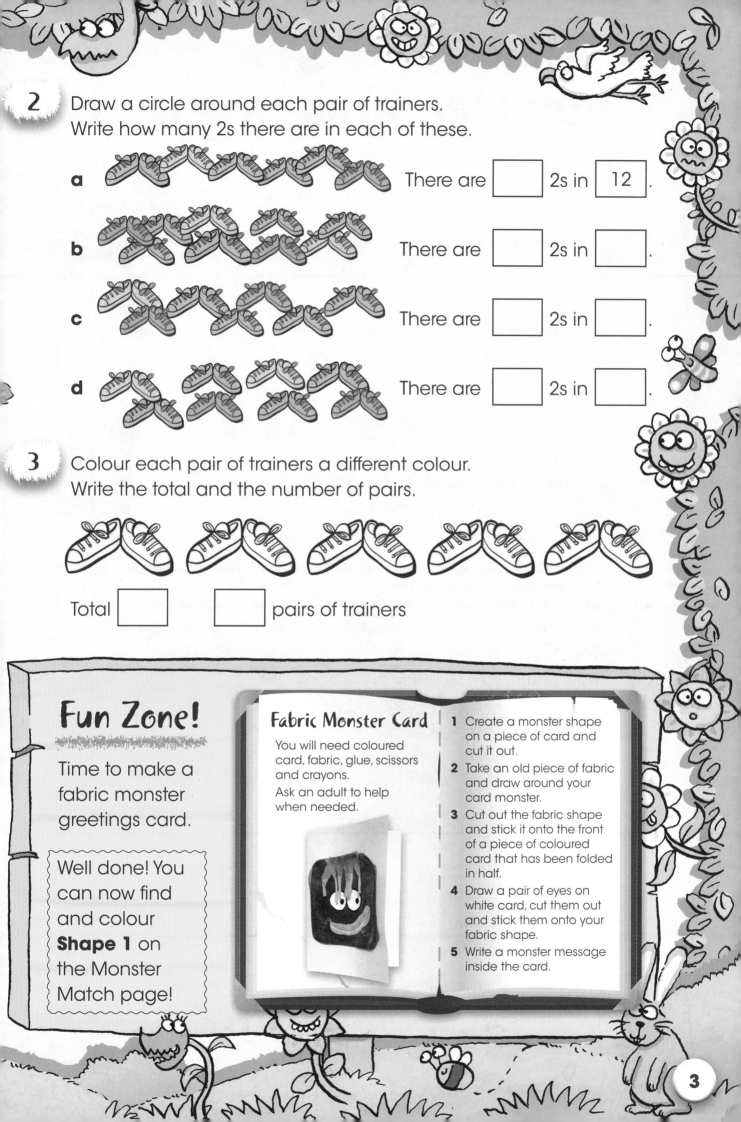 There are ☐ 2s in 12.

b There are ☐ 2s in ☐.

c There are ☐ 2s in ☐.

d There are ☐ 2s in ☐.

3 Colour each pair of trainers a different colour.
Write the total and the number of pairs.

Total ☐ ☐ pairs of trainers

Fun Zone!

Time to make a fabric monster greetings card.

Well done! You can now find and colour **Shape 1** on the Monster Match page!

Fabric Monster Card

You will need coloured card, fabric, glue, scissors and crayons.

Ask an adult to help when needed.

1 Create a monster shape on a piece of card and cut it out.
2 Take an old piece of fabric and draw around your card monster.
3 Cut out the fabric shape and stick it onto the front of a piece of coloured card that has been folded in half.
4 Draw a pair of eyes on white card, cut them out and stick them onto your fabric shape.
5 Write a monster message inside the card.

Monster Grouping in 5s

Kora and Litmus are making glasses of orange juice for their friends.
Each glass needs 5 oranges.
They want to know how many glasses they can make.

They put the oranges into groups of 5 and then count the groups.

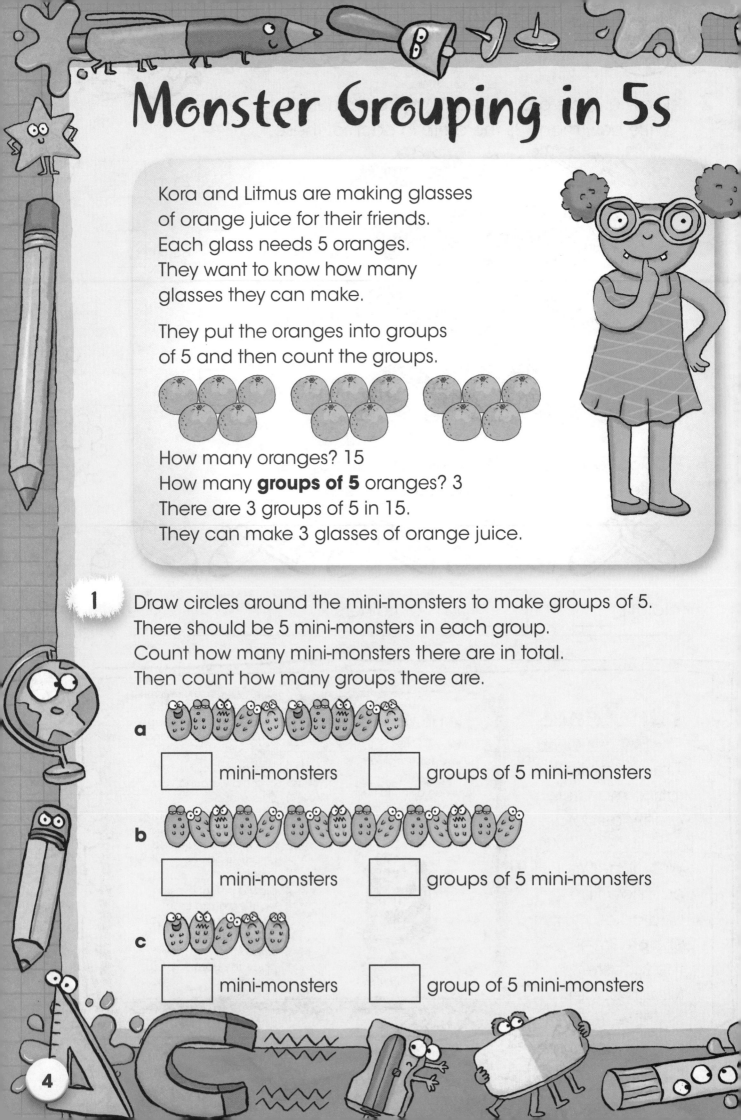

How many oranges? 15
How many **groups of 5** oranges? 3
There are 3 groups of 5 in 15.
They can make 3 glasses of orange juice.

1 Draw circles around the mini-monsters to make groups of 5.
There should be 5 mini-monsters in each group.
Count how many mini-monsters there are in total.
Then count how many groups there are.

a

☐ mini-monsters ☐ groups of 5 mini-monsters

b

☐ mini-monsters ☐ groups of 5 mini-monsters

c

☐ mini-monsters ☐ group of 5 mini-monsters

2 Here are some squints.
Draw circles around groups of 5.
Write how many 5s there are in total.

a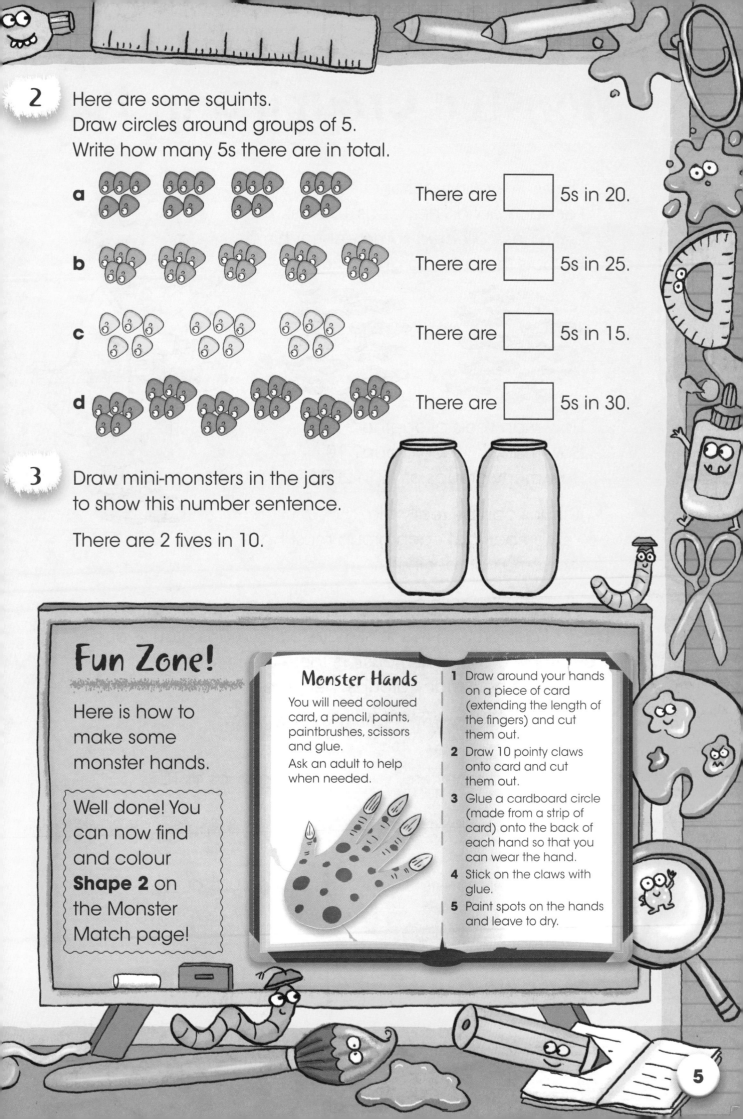

There are ☐ 5s in 20.

b

There are ☐ 5s in 25.

c

There are ☐ 5s in 15.

d

There are ☐ 5s in 30.

3 Draw mini-monsters in the jars
to show this number sentence.

There are 2 fives in 10.

Fun Zone!

Here is how to
make some
monster hands.

Well done! You
can now find
and colour
Shape 2 on
the Monster
Match page!

Monster Hands

You will need coloured
card, a pencil, paints,
paintbrushes, scissors
and glue.

Ask an adult to help
when needed.

1 Draw around your hands
on a piece of card
(extending the length of
the fingers) and cut
them out.
2 Draw 10 pointy claws
onto card and cut
them out.
3 Glue a cardboard circle
(made from a strip of
card) onto the back of
each hand so that you
can wear the hand.
4 Stick on the claws with
glue.
5 Paint spots on the hands
and leave to dry.

Monster Grouping in 10s

Litmus is making potions.
For each potion he needs 10 eels.
Gran has collected some eels for him.
He puts the eels into **groups of 10**.

How many eels altogether? 20
How many in each group? 10
How many groups of 10 in 20? 2

Groups can be really big.
Remember that each group must have
the same number in it!

1 Draw circles around the mini-monsters to make groups of 10.
Count how many mini-monsters there are in total.
Then count how many groups there are.

a

☐ mini-monsters ☐ groups of 10

b

☐ mini-monsters ☐ groups of 10

c

☐ mini-monsters ☐ group of 10

2 Draw circles around the tubes to make groups of 10.
Count how many groups of ten there are in total.

a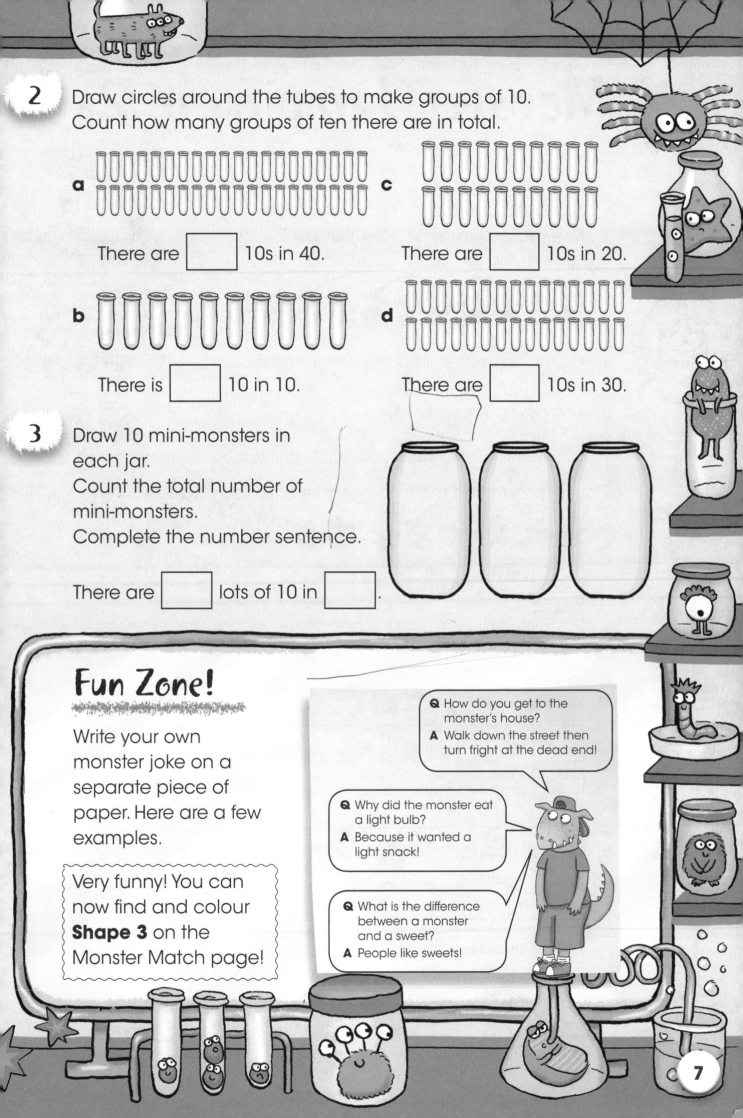

There are ☐ 10s in 40.

b

There is ☐ 10 in 10.

c

There are ☐ 10s in 20.

d

There are ☐ 10s in 30.

3 Draw 10 mini-monsters in each jar.
Count the total number of mini-monsters.
Complete the number sentence.

There are ☐ lots of 10 in ☐.

Fun Zone!

Write your own monster joke on a separate piece of paper. Here are a few examples.

Very funny! You can now find and colour **Shape 3** on the Monster Match page!

Q How do you get to the monster's house?
A Walk down the street then turn fright at the dead end!

Q Why did the monster eat a light bulb?
A Because it wanted a light snack!

Q What is the difference between a monster and a sweet?
A People like sweets!

Monster Jumping in 2s

It has been raining.
Fizz loves jumping in muddy puddles.
She makes jumps of 2 to count in 2s.
Look at the jumps.

0 1 2 3 4 5 6 7 8 9 10

Count on in 2s to find the next number.
2, 4, 6, 8, ?
The next number is 10.

1 Count in 2s to find the total number of muddy puddles.

a

$\boxed{2}$ + $\boxed{2}$ + $\boxed{}$ + $\boxed{}$

$\boxed{}$ puddles altogether.

b

$\boxed{}$ + $\boxed{}$ + $\boxed{}$ + $\boxed{}$ + $\boxed{}$ + $\boxed{}$

$\boxed{}$ puddles altogether.

c

$\boxed{}$ + $\boxed{}$ + $\boxed{}$ + $\boxed{}$ + $\boxed{}$ + $\boxed{}$ + $\boxed{}$ + $\boxed{}$

$\boxed{}$ puddles altogether.

2 Write the next number for each of these.

a 0 2 4 ☐   **e** 18 16 14 ☐

b 4 6 8 ☐   **f** 14 12 10 ☐

c 2 4 6 ☐   **g** 16 14 12 ☐

d 6 8 10 ☐   **h** 12 10 8 ☐

3 Count in 2s to find the missing numbers.

a | 2 | 4 | 6 | | | | | | 18 |

b | | | 8 | 10 | 12 | 14 | | | |

c | 20 | 18 | 16 | | | | | | 4 |

d | | 10 | 12 | | | | 20 | | |

Fun Zone!

Draw your own monster faces.

Marvellous monsters! You can now find and colour **Shape 4** on the Monster Match page!

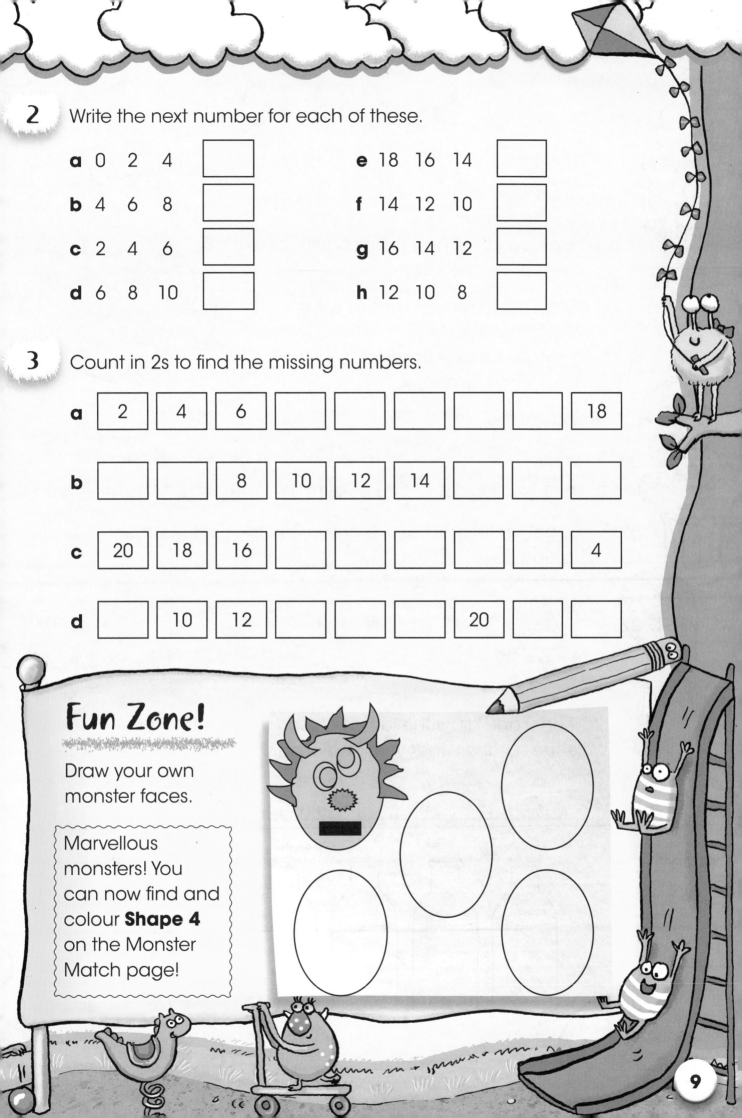

9

5s and 10s

Fizz is looking after Nano.
Nano is very hungry!
Fizz is counting how many bottles of milk there are in the fridge.

Counting in groups means we can find totals quickly.
It is called **multiplication**.
We use the symbol ✖.

Look at the jumps.

| 0 | 1 | 2 | 3 | 4 | **5** | 6 | 7 | 8 | 9 | **10** | 11 | 12 | 13 | 14 | **15** | 16 | 17 | 18 | 19 | **20** |

Count on the next group of 5 to find the next number to land on… 20.
Finish the jump to land on 20.
5 + 5 + 5 + 5 = 20
4 lots of 5 = 20
4 ✖ 5 = 20

1 Start on 0 and draw the jumps of 5 on the number line.
Write the numbers that you land on in the bottles.

0 1 2 3 4 5 6 7 8 9 10 11 12 13 14 15 16 17 18 19 20 21 22 23 24 25 26 27 28 29 30

5

2 Write the missing numbers and complete the number sentences below.

| 0 | 5 | 10 | 15 | 20 | 25 | 30 |

5 + 5 + 5 + 5 + 5 + 5 = 30

6 lots of 5 = 30   6 × 5 = 30

3 Look at the grid below.
Start at 1 and colour the first group of 10 green.
Choose a different colour for the next group of 10.
Keep going until all the numbers are coloured.

1	2	3	4	5	6	7	8	9	10
11	12	13	14	15	16	17	18	19	20
21	22	23	24	25	26	27	28	29	30
31	32	33	34	35	36	37	38	39	40
41	42	43	44	45	46	47	48	49	50

How many groups of 10 are there? ☐

Look at the last number of each group.

Write them all here.　| 10 | ☐ | ☐ | ☐ | ☐ |

Fun Zone!

Here is an acrostic poem about Nano. On a separate piece of paper, write a similar poem for your own name.

Naughty

Amazing

Noisy

Original

Well done! You can now find and colour **Shape 5** on the Monster Match page!

Groups of Creatures

Fizz and Poggo are in the cave looking for monster creatures.

Many objects show patterns and groups of numbers.
Look at these wonderful bats!

A bat has 2 wings.
How many wings on 4 bats? 8
We can write this as 4 lots of 2 equals 8.

4 × 2 = 8

1 Write the number of objects in each group.
Write the total.

a | 1 | frog = | 5 | spots 1 × 5 = | 5 |

 | 3 | frogs = | 15 | spots 3 × 5 = | ~~10~~ 15 |

b | 1 | lizard = | 2 | eyes 1 × 2 = | |

 | 4 | lizards = | 8 | eyes 4 × 2 = | 8 |

c | 1 | snake = | 10 | stripes 1 × 10 = | |

 | 2 | snakes = | 20 | stripes 2 × 10 = | |

d | 1 | spider = | 2 | teeth 1 × 2 = | |

 | 6 | spiders = | 12 | teeth 6 × 2 = | |

2 A lomp has 5 eyes.
Write the number sentence.
Work out how many eyes there are altogether.

a $\boxed{3} \times \boxed{5} = \boxed{}$

b $\boxed{} \times \boxed{5} = \boxed{}$

c $\boxed{} \times \boxed{} = \boxed{}$

d $\boxed{} \times \boxed{} = \boxed{}$

e $\boxed{} \times \boxed{} = \boxed{}$

3 A caterpillar has 10 legs, a frog has 5 spots and a snail has 2 eyes.
Write the number sentence and work out the total.

a $\boxed{} \times \boxed{10} = \boxed{}$

b $\boxed{} \times \boxed{5} = \boxed{}$

c $\boxed{9} \times \boxed{} = \boxed{}$

Fun Zone!

It is time to make a bat.

That is a great bat! You can now find and colour **Shape 6** on the Monster Match page!

Bat

You will need a cardboard tube, black paint, black card, white paper, glue, scissors and crayons.

Ask an adult to help when needed.

1 Paint the cardboard tube and leave to dry. Make two cuts down either side of the tube.

2 Cut the black card into the shape of bat wings.

3 Draw some eyes and some pointed teeth on the white paper and cut them out.

4 Stick on the eyes and the teeth.

5 Use a white crayon to draw on the wings.

6 Push the wings down the cuts in the tube.

Monster Challenge 1

1 Draw a circle around groups of 2.

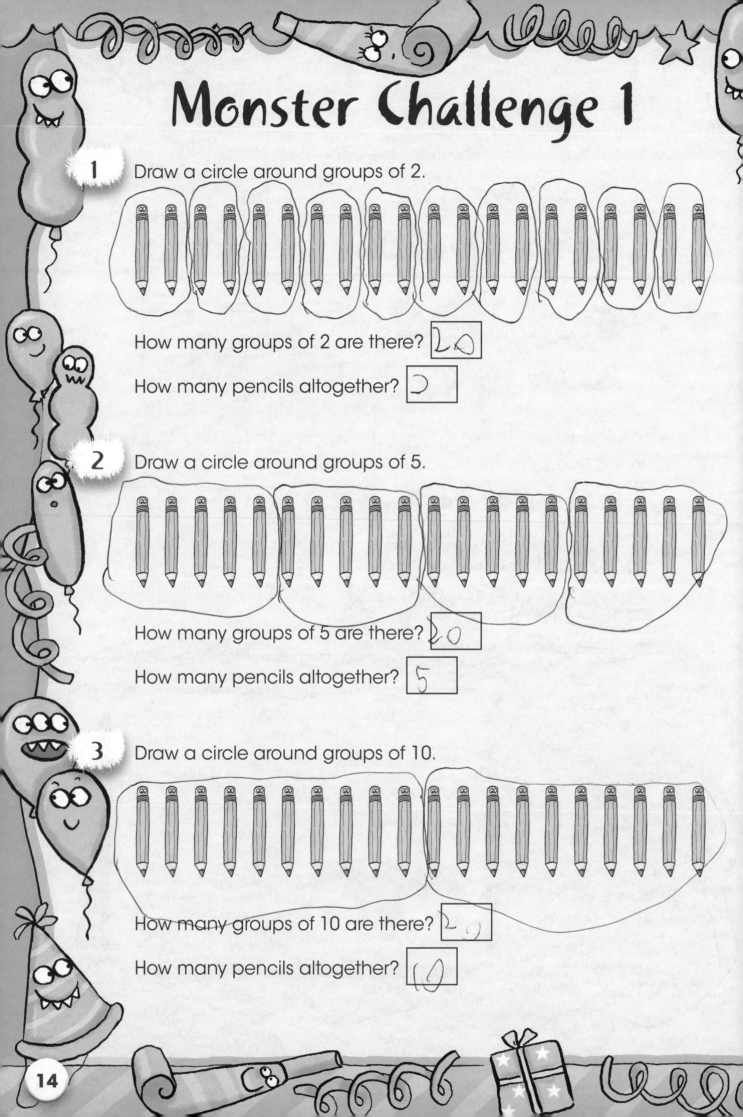

How many groups of 2 are there? ☐ 10

How many pencils altogether? ☐ 2

2 Draw a circle around groups of 5.

How many groups of 5 are there? ☐ 20

How many pencils altogether? ☐ 5

3 Draw a circle around groups of 10.

How many groups of 10 are there? ☐ 20

How many pencils altogether? ☐ 10

4

Fill in the missing numbers to complete the sequence.

a

| 10 | 12 | 14 | 16 | 18 | 20 |

b

| 10 | 8 | 6 | 4 | 2 | 0 |

c

| 20 | 18 | 16 | 14 | 12 |

5

Multiply the numbers and write them in the new grid.

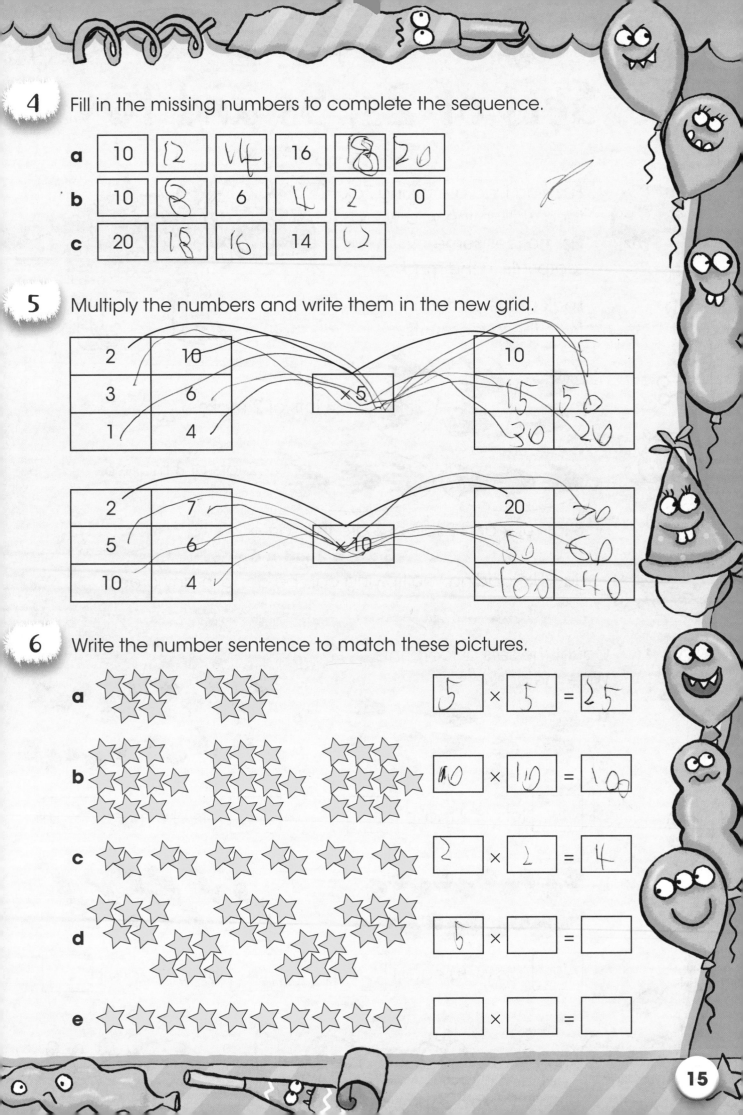

2	10
3	6
1	4

×5

10	5
15	50
30	20

2	7
5	6
10	4

×10

20	70
50	60
100	40

6

Write the number sentence to match these pictures.

a

$5 \times 5 = 25$

b

$10 \times 10 = 100$

c

$2 \times 2 = 4$

d

$5 \times \boxed{} = \boxed{}$

e

$\boxed{} \times \boxed{} = \boxed{}$

Sets of 2s, 5s and 10s

Fizz and Dad are taking Zak for a walk in the wild wood. Fizz notices some footprints in the mud.

Look at the patterns made from these footprints.

3 lots of 2 make 6.

2 lots of 3 make 6.

3 lots of 2 and 2 lots of 3 are the same.

3 × 2 = 2 × 3 = 6

Just like adding, multiplying can be done in any order.

1 Count the sets of footprints.
Write the answers.

a

[ ] lots of 2 make [ ]

c

[ ] lots of 5 make [ ]

b

[ ] lots of 10 equal [ ]

d

[ ] lots of 5 equal [ ]

2 Colour these leaves to show the groups.

a 5 lots of 2 leaves

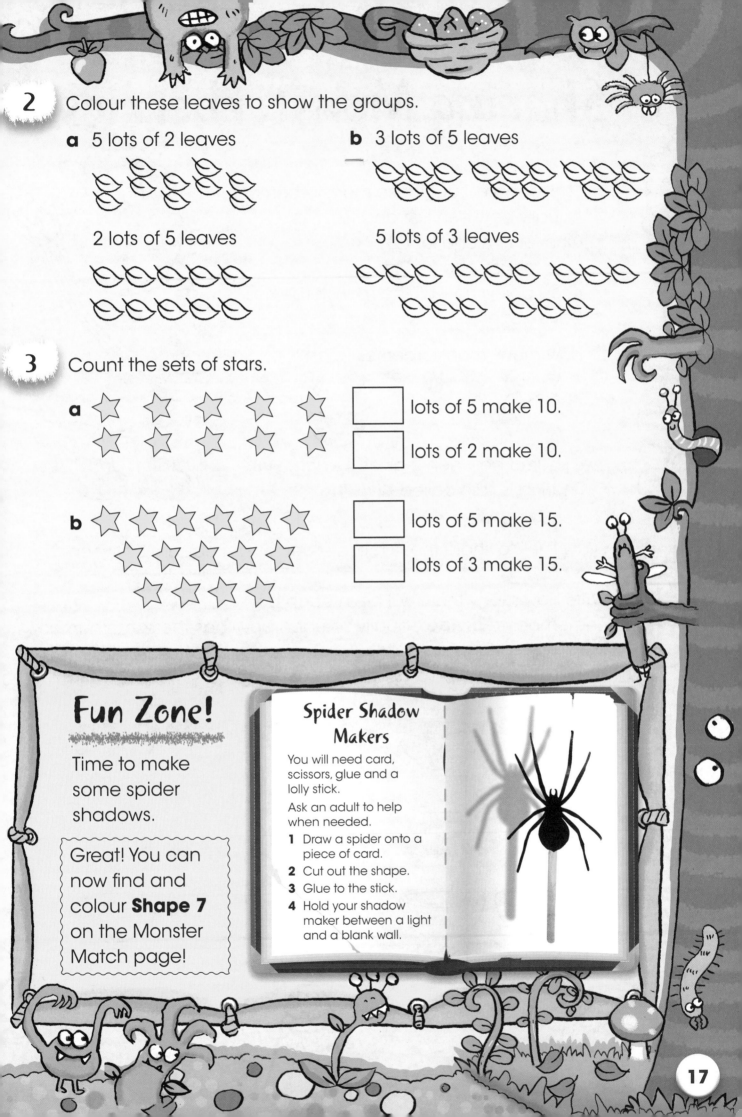

2 lots of 5 leaves

b 3 lots of 5 leaves

5 lots of 3 leaves

3 Count the sets of stars.

a

☐ lots of 5 make 10.

☐ lots of 2 make 10.

b

☐ lots of 5 make 15.

☐ lots of 3 make 15.

Fun Zone!

Time to make some spider shadows.

Great! You can now find and colour **Shape 7** on the Monster Match page!

Spider Shadow Makers

You will need card, scissors, glue and a lolly stick.

Ask an adult to help when needed.

1 Draw a spider onto a piece of card.
2 Cut out the shape.
3 Glue to the stick.
4 Hold your shadow maker between a light and a blank wall.

Sharing Monsterberries

I have shared out these monsterberries equally between Fizz and Tizz.
One for Fizz, one for Tizz,
One for Fizz, one for Tizz…
Keep going until all the monsterberries have gone!

How many monsterberries each?

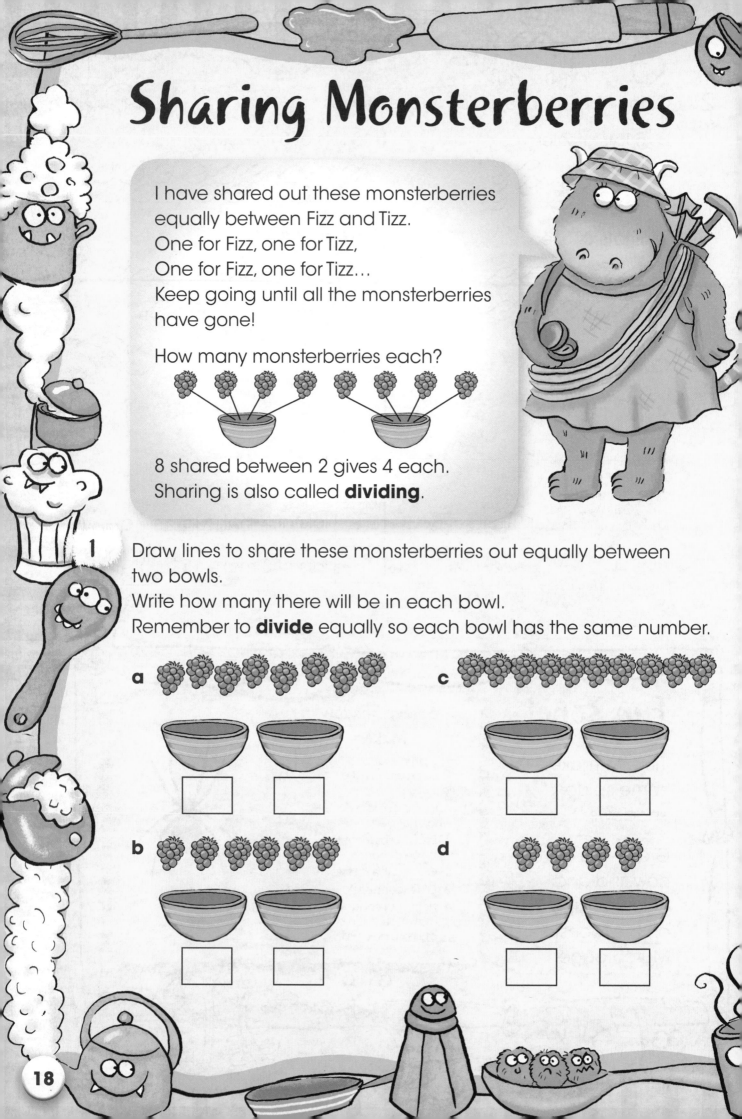

8 shared between 2 gives 4 each.
Sharing is also called **dividing**.

1 Draw lines to share these monsterberries out equally between two bowls.
Write how many there will be in each bowl.
Remember to **divide** equally so each bowl has the same number.

a

c

b

d

2 Draw lines to share the shopping out equally between two baskets.

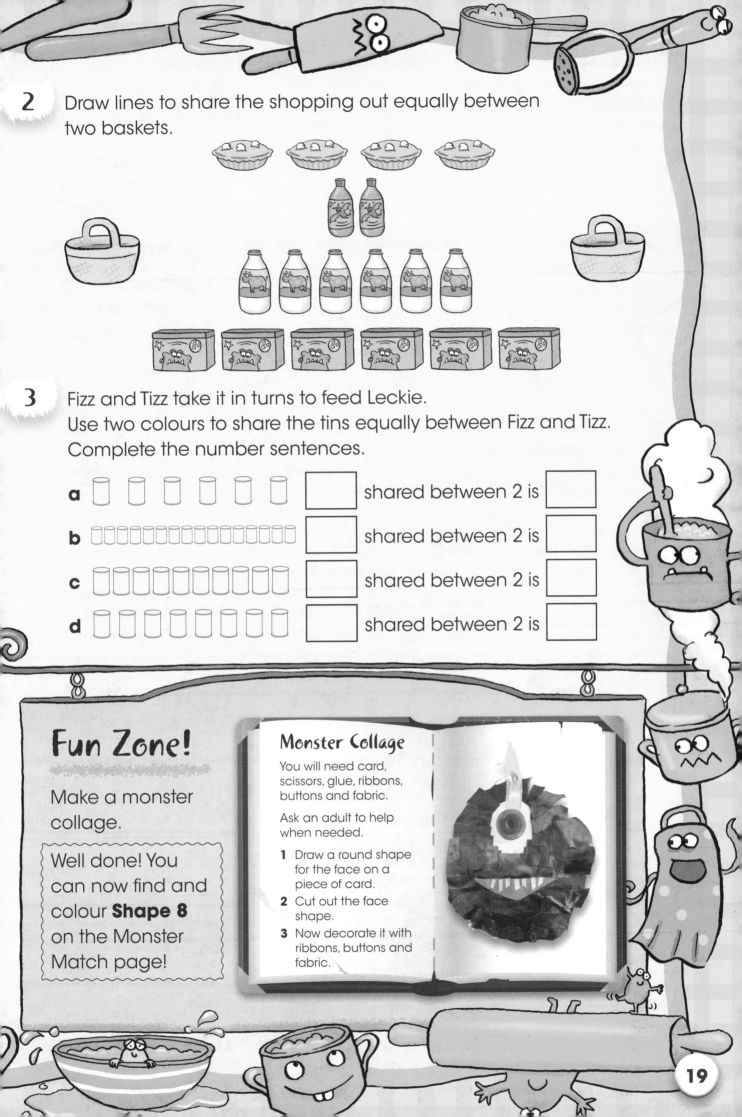

3 Fizz and Tizz take it in turns to feed Leckie.
Use two colours to share the tins equally between Fizz and Tizz.
Complete the number sentences.

a ☐ ☐ ☐ ☐ ☐ ☐   [   ] shared between 2 is [   ]

b ☐☐☐☐☐☐☐☐☐☐☐☐☐   [   ] shared between 2 is [   ]

c ☐☐☐☐☐☐☐☐☐☐   [   ] shared between 2 is [   ]

d ☐☐☐☐☐☐☐☐   [   ] shared between 2 is [   ]

Fun Zone!

Make a monster collage.

Well done! You can now find and colour **Shape 8** on the Monster Match page!

Monster Collage

You will need card, scissors, glue, ribbons, buttons and fabric.

Ask an adult to help when needed.

1 Draw a round shape for the face on a piece of card.
2 Cut out the face shape.
3 Now decorate it with ribbons, buttons and fabric.

Sharing 5s and 10s

I am sorting out my photo albums.
I have 15 photos.
I want to share these photos between 5 albums.
Can you check that I have shared equally?

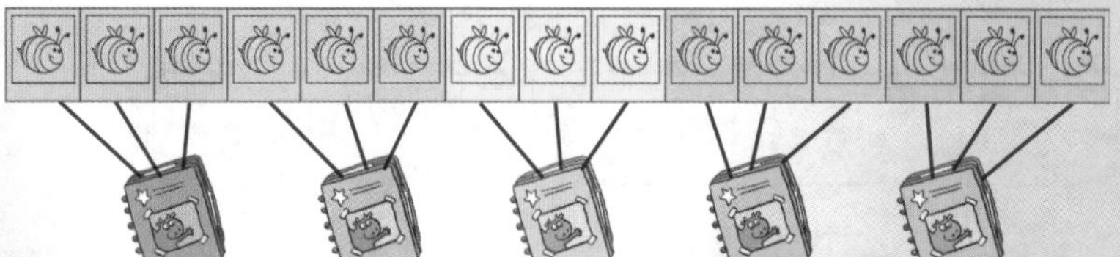

15 shared between 5 gives 3 each.
Yes, that's right!

1 Draw lines to share the photos equally between the albums.
Colour the photos to match the albums.
Complete the number sentence.

a

10 shared between 5 is ☐ each.

b

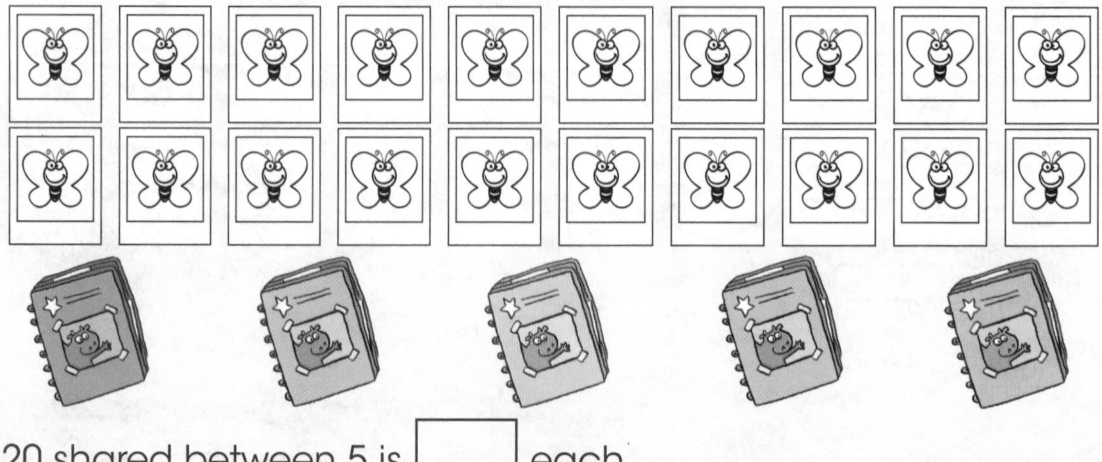

20 shared between 5 is ☐ each.

2 Complete these number sentences.

a 20 photos shared between 10 albums is ☐ photos each.

b 15 photos shared between 5 albums is ☐ photos each.

c 30 photos shared between 10 albums is ☐ photos each.

3 Draw lines to share these photos equally between the albums.

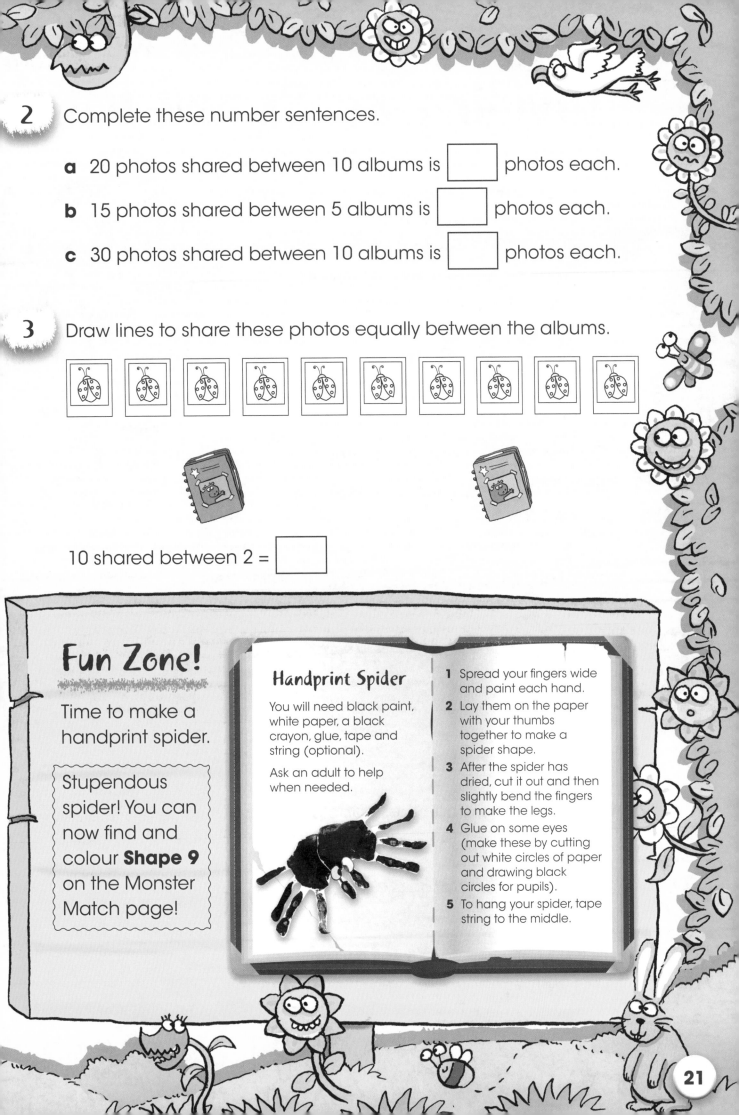

10 shared between 2 = ☐

Fun Zone!

Time to make a handprint spider.

Stupendous spider! You can now find and colour **Shape 9** on the Monster Match page!

Handprint Spider

You will need black paint, white paper, a black crayon, glue, tape and string (optional).

Ask an adult to help when needed.

1 Spread your fingers wide and paint each hand.

2 Lay them on the paper with your thumbs together to make a spider shape.

3 After the spider has dried, cut it out and then slightly bend the fingers to make the legs.

4 Glue on some eyes (make these by cutting out white circles of paper and drawing black circles for pupils).

5 To hang your spider, tape string to the middle.

Dividing 2s, 5s and 10s

Gran is collecting apples to make apple and monsterberry pies.
She wants to make 2 pies.

She puts the apples into groups of 2 and counts how many groups.

Gran knows 5 groups of 2 means 5 apples in each pie.

Division is shown by the symbol ÷.

10 divided by 2 = 5
10 ÷ 2 = 5

1 Draw circles to group these toadstools into 2s.
Then count the groups and complete the number sentences.

a

8 = ☐ groups of 2

8 ÷ 2 = ☐

b

6 = ☐ groups of 2

6 ÷ 2 = ☐

2 Draw circles to group these apples into 5s.
Then count the groups and complete the number sentences.

a

☐ groups of 5

10 ÷ 5 = ☐

b

☐ groups of 5

15 ÷ ☐ = ☐

3 Draw circles to show the groups of eggs.
Complete the number sentences.

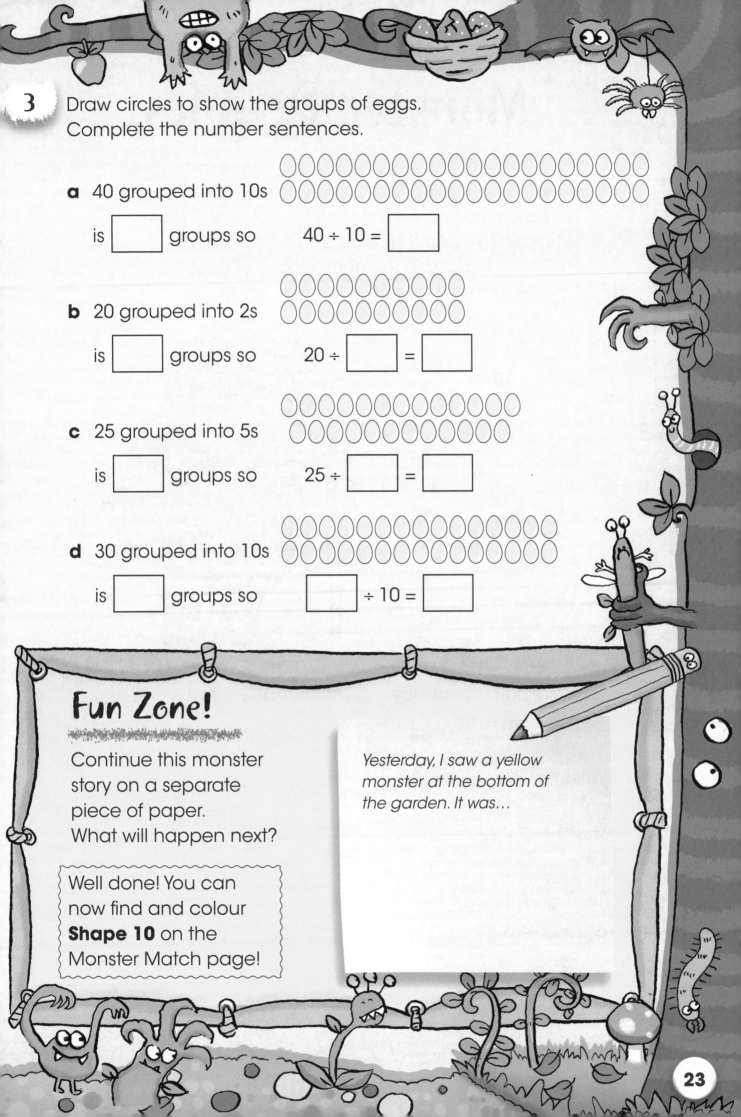

a 40 grouped into 10s

is ☐ groups so   40 ÷ 10 = ☐

b 20 grouped into 2s

is ☐ groups so   20 ÷ ☐ = ☐

c 25 grouped into 5s

is ☐ groups so   25 ÷ ☐ = ☐

d 30 grouped into 10s

is ☐ groups so   ☐ ÷ 10 = ☐

Fun Zone!

Continue this monster
story on a separate
piece of paper.
What will happen next?

*Yesterday, I saw a yellow
monster at the bottom of
the garden. It was…*

Well done! You can
now find and colour
Shape 10 on the
Monster Match page!

Monster Doubles

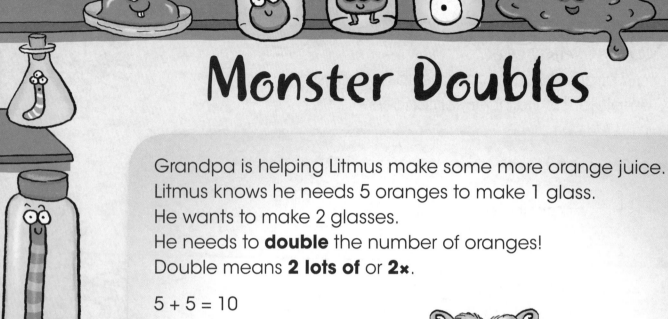

Grandpa is helping Litmus make some more orange juice.
Litmus knows he needs 5 oranges to make 1 glass.
He wants to make 2 glasses.
He needs to **double** the number of oranges!
Double means **2 lots of** or **2×**.

5 + 5 = 10
Double 5 is 10.
2 × 5 = 10

1		2
2		4
3		6
4		8
5	doubled	10
6		12
7		14
8		16
9		18
10		20

Try to learn the doubles of the numbers 1 to 10.

1 Write the answers to these.

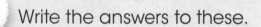

a double 2 = ☐   **d** double 5 = ☐

b double 4 = ☐   **e** double 3 = ☐

c double 6 = ☐   **f** double 1 = ☐

2 Draw spots on the second dice to match those on the first one.
Then write the totals.
The first one has been done for you.

a   [⚂ dice: 3 spots]   [dice: 3 spots] $\boxed{3}$ + $\boxed{3}$ = $\boxed{6}$

b   [dice: 4 spots] $\boxed{}$ $\boxed{}$ + $\boxed{}$ = $\boxed{}$

c   [dice: 3 spots] $\boxed{}$ $\boxed{}$ + $\boxed{}$ = $\boxed{}$

d   [dice: 1 spot] $\boxed{}$ $\boxed{}$ + $\boxed{}$ = $\boxed{}$

e   [dice: 6 spots] $\boxed{}$ $\boxed{}$ + $\boxed{}$ = $\boxed{}$

f   [dice: 2 spots] $\boxed{}$ $\boxed{}$ + $\boxed{}$ = $\boxed{}$

3 Draw a line to join each domino total to its number double.

8	10	2	6	4	20	14	12

Fun Zone!

Draw faces, arms and legs to turn these shapes into monsters.

Scary monsters!
You can now find and colour **Shape 11** on the Monster Match page!

Halves and Quarters

The Professor is teaching Fizz about fractions.

Sharing into **2** equal groups is called **halving**.

1 half can be written as:

1 ←—(this means 1 part)

2 ←—(this means shared into 2 equal parts)

We can halve shapes and numbers.

1 half of 8 = 4

8 ÷ 2 = 4

Sharing into **4** equal groups is called **quartering**.

1 quarter can be written as:

1 ←—(this means 1 equal part)

4 ←—(this means shared into 4 equal parts)

We can quarter shapes and numbers too.

1 quarter of 8 = 2

8 ÷ 4 = 2

1 Colour 1 half of each shape yellow.
Complete the number sentence.

☐
— of each shape is coloured yellow.
☐

2 Colour 1 quarter of each shape red.
Complete the number sentence.

◻—— of each shape is
coloured red.

3 Draw rings around these rulers to put them into two
equal groups.
Count the rulers in one group and complete the
number sentences.

a

Half of 6 is ◻

6 ÷ 2 = ◻

b

Half of 10 is ◻

10 ÷ 2 = ◻

Fun Zone!

Find the five
differences between
the two pictures
of Fizz.

Monsterific! You
can now find and
colour **Shape 12**
on the Monster
Match page!

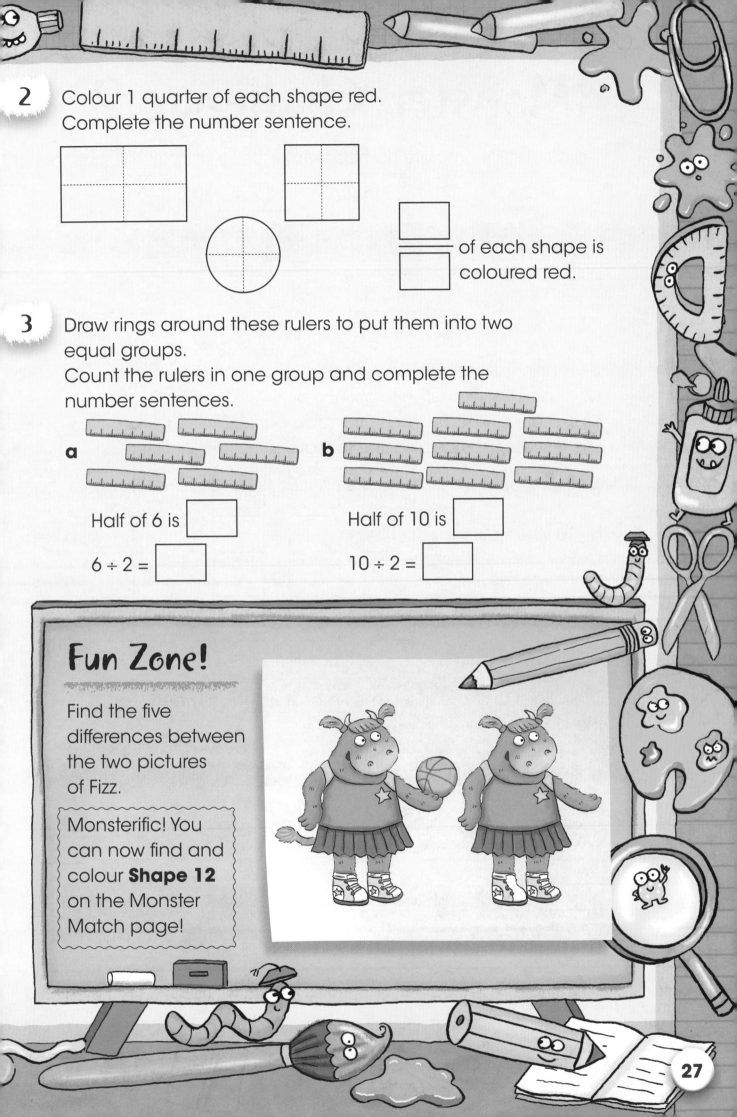

Monster Challenge 2

1 Colour the incomplete number sentences to match the answers.

2×5	2×6	2×4	5×2

10	8	20	12

10×2	4×2	2×10	6×2

2 Grandpa is fixing two new wheels onto each bike.
He shares the wheels into groups of two.
Work out how many bikes Grandpa can fix.
The first one has been done for you.

a 6 wheels $\boxed{6} \div \boxed{2} = \boxed{3}$ $\boxed{3}$ bikes

b 10 wheels $\boxed{10} \div \boxed{} = \boxed{}$ $\boxed{}$ bikes

c 16 wheels $\boxed{} \div \boxed{2} = \boxed{}$ $\boxed{}$ bikes

d 8 wheels $\boxed{} \div \boxed{} = \boxed{}$ $\boxed{}$ bikes

3 Draw lines to share these mini-monsters equally between the baskets.

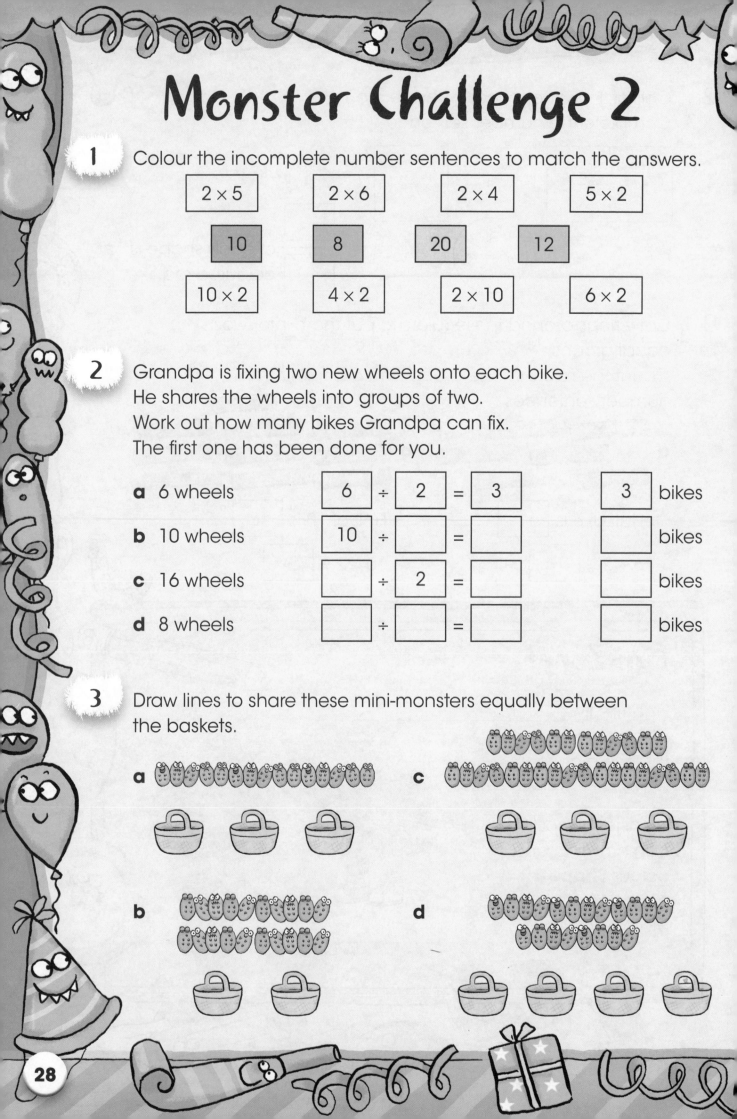

a

b

c

d

4 Colour the balloon with the right answer.

a 20 ÷ 5   (3) (4) (5)   **c** 90 ÷ 10   (8) (9) (10)

b 14 ÷ 2   (8) (7) (6)   **d** 18 ÷ 2   (7) (8) (9)

5 Work out the total if each dart scores double the number.

a   [3] × [2] = [ ]

b   [ ] × [2] = [ ]

c   [ ] × [2] = [ ]

6 Colour half of the mini-monsters in each jar red.
Now colour yellow half of the mini-monsters that are not coloured red.
Tip: half of a half is $\frac{1}{4}$.
Complete the number sentences.

a

Half of 16 is [ ]

b

Half of 8 is [ ]

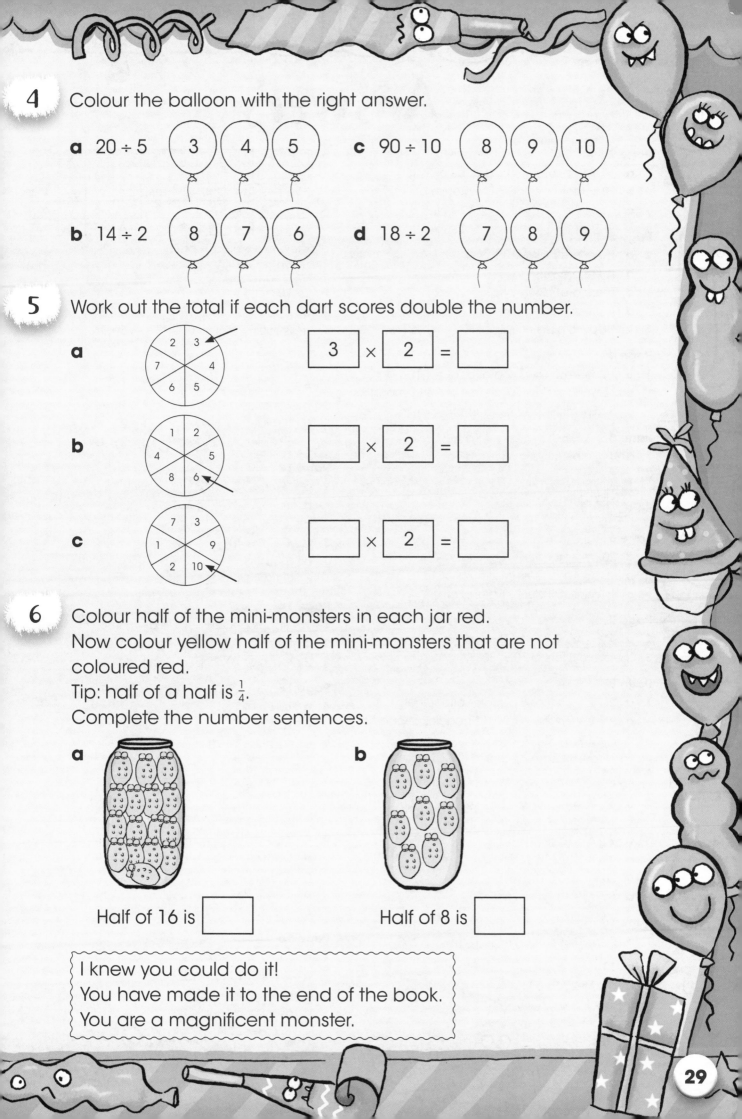

Answers

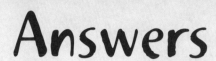

Page 2

1   **a**   10 flies in total with 5 groups of 2

   b   12 spiders in total with 6 groups of 2

   c   6 frogs in total with 3 groups of 2

Page 3

2   **a**   There are 6 2s in 12.

   b   There are 9 2s in 18.

   c   There are 7 2s in 14.

   d   There are 8 2s in 16.

3   Total 10   5 pairs of trainers

Page 4

1   **a**   10 mini-monsters   2 groups of 5 mini-monsters

   b   15 mini-monsters   3 groups of 5 mini-monsters

   c   5 mini-monsters   1 group of 5 mini-monsters

Page 5

2   **a** 4   **b** 5   **c** 3   **d** 6

3

Page 6

1   **a**   20 mini-monsters   2 groups of 10

   b   40 mini-monsters   4 groups of 10

   c   10 mini-monsters   1 group of 10

Page 7

2   **a** 4   **b** 1   **c** 2   **d** 3

3   There are 3 lots of 10 in 30.

Page 8

1   **a**   2 + 2 + 2 + 2   8 puddles altogether

   b   2 + 2 + 2 + 2 + 2 + 2   12 puddles altogether

   c   2 + 2 + 2 + 2 + 2 + 2 + 2 + 2

    16 puddles altogether

Page 9

2   **a** 6   **c** 8   **e** 12   **g** 10

   b 10   **d** 12   **f** 8   **h** 6

3   **a**   2 4 6 8 10 12 14 16 18

   b   4 6 8 10 12 14 16 18 20

   c   20 18 16 14 12 10 8 6 4

   d   8 10 12 14 16 18 20 22 24

Page 10

1   5 10 15 20 25 30

Page 11

2   0 5 10 15 20 25 30

   5 + 5 + 5 + 5 + 5 + 5 = 30

   6 lots of 5 = 30   6 × 5 = 30

3

1	2	3	4	5	6	7	8	9	10
11	12	13	14	15	16	17	18	19	20
21	22	23	24	25	26	27	28	29	30
31	32	33	34	35	36	37	38	39	40
41	42	43	44	45	46	47	48	49	50

There are 5 groups of 10.

10, 20, 30, 40, 50

Page 12

1   **a**   1 frog = 5 spots   1 × 5 = 5

     3 frogs = 15 spots   3 × 5 = 15

   b   1 lizard = 2 eyes   1 × 2 = 2

     4 lizards = 8 eyes   4 × 2 = 8

   c   1 snake = 10 stripes   1 × 10 = 10

     2 snakes = 20 stripes   2 × 10 = 20

   d   1 spider = 2 teeth   1 × 2 = 2

     6 spiders = 12 teeth   6 × 2 = 12

Page 13

2   **a**   3 × 5 = 15;   **d**   8 × 5 = 40;

   b   6 × 5 = 30;   **e**   4 × 5 = 20;

   c   2 × 5 = 10

3   **a**   4 × 10 = 40

   b   6 × 5 = 30

   c   9 × 2 = 18

Page 14

1   10 groups of 2, 20 pencils altogether

2   4 groups of 5, 20 pencils altogether

3   2 groups of 10, 20 pencils altogether

Page 15

4   **a**   10 12 14 16 18 20

   b   10 8 6 4 2 0

   c   20 18 16 14 12

5

10	50
15	30
5	20

20	70
50	60
100	40

6   **a**   2 × 5 = 10

   b   3 × 10 = 30

   c   6 × 2 = 12

   d   5 × 5 = 25

   e   1 × 10 = 10 or 10 × 1 = 10

Page 16

1   **a**   5 lots of 2 make 10

   b   2 lots of 10 equal 20

   c   4 lots of 5 make 20

   d   6 lots of 5 equal 30

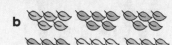

Page 17

2 a   **b**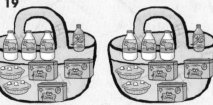

3 a 2 lots of 5 make 10.   5 lots of 2 make 10.

   b 3 lots of 5 make 15.   5 lots of 3 make 15.

Page 18

1 a 4 monsterberries in each bowl.

   b 3 monsterberries in each bowl.

   c 5 monsterberries in each bowl.

   d 2 monsterberries in each bowl.

Page 19

2

3 a 6 shared between 2 is 3

   b 16 shared between 2 is 8

   c 10 shared between 2 is 5

   d 8 shared between 2 is 4

Page 20

1 a

10 shared between 5 is 2 each

   b

20 shared between 5 is 4 each

Page 21

2 a 2   **b** 3   **c** 3

3

10 shared between 2 = 5

Page 22

1 a 8 = 4 groups $8 \div 2 = 4$

   b 6 = 3 groups $6 \div 2 = 3$

2 a 2 groups $10 \div 5 = 2$

   b 3 groups $15 \div 5 = 3$

Page 23

3 a 4 groups $40 \div 10 = 4$

   b 10 groups $20 \div 2 = 10$

   c 5 groups $25 \div 5 = 5$

   d 3 groups $30 \div 10 = 3$

Page 24

1 a 4   **b** 8   **c** 12   **d** 10   **e** 6   **f** 2

Page 25

2 a $3 + 3 = 6$

   b $5 + 5 = 10$

   c $4 + 4 = 8$

   d $1 + 1 = 2$

   e $6 + 6 = 12$

   f $2 + 2 = 4$

3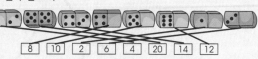

8   10   2   6   4   20   14   12

Page 26

1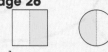

$\frac{1}{2}$ of each shape is coloured.

Page 27

2

$\frac{1}{4}$ of each shape is coloured.

3 a Half of 6 is 3 $6 \div 2 = 3$

   b Half of 10 is 5 $10 \div 2 = 5$

Fun Zone

Page 28

1 red: 2×5 and 5×2; green: 2×4 and 4×2; yellow: 10×2 and 2×10; blue: 2×6 and 6×2

2 a $6 \div 2 = 3$ 3 bikes

   b $10 \div 2 = 5$ 5 bikes

   c $16 \div 2 = 8$ 8 bikes

   d $8 \div 2 = 4$ 4 bikes

3 a 5 mini-monsters in each basket

   b 10 mini-monsters in each basket

   c 10 mini-monsters in each basket

   d 5 mini-monsters in each basket

Page 29

4 a 4   **b** 7   **c** 9   **d** 9

5 a $3 \times 2 = 6$

   b $6 \times 2 = 12$

   c $10 \times 2 = 20$

6 a 8 mini-monsters coloured red

     4 mini-monsters coloured yellow

     Half of 16 is 8

   b 4 mini-monsters coloured red

     2 mini-monsters coloured yellow

     Half of 8 is 4

Monster Match

Each time you complete a topic in this book, you will be awarded a shape number.

Find and colour the shapes in the picture of Fizz that match the numbers you have been given.

As you work through the book you will gradually see Fizz come to life!